Introduction

Snakes are among the most fascinating animals on earth, and are either loved or feared by all. Snakes hold a special place in our history, and throughout time have been symbols of health, caution, freedom, death, evil and more. Many people fear snakes because they are mysterious, some are venomous, and all are predators. The same attributes that repel some people from snakes, lure others closer.

Snakes can make intriguing pets that are easily maintained when cared for properly. Selecting the proper snake species will be important in making a decision about which snake is best for your household. The larger species of snakes are only suited for large zoo style enclosures maintained by the most experienced keepers. There are several snakes that are available that do not make good pets for beginners. We encourage anyone interested in getting a snake to research the needs of the species you wish to keep, and to be prepared to care for the snake throughout its life. If you are considering a snake as a pet, this book will help guide you in the proper selection, care, and maintenance of many popular pet snakes.

DONT TREAD ON ME

The Gadsden Flag is a historical American Flag from the Revolutionary War, and considered by some, one of the first American Flags. The rattlesnake symbolizes the true courage of the American Revolution. Snakes represent vigilance because they do not have eyelids, and therefore never blink. "She never begins an attack, nor, when once engaged, ever surrenders."

-Benjamin Franklin, 1775

Y0-AQP-563

Is a Snake the Right Pet for You?

There are many different kinds of snakes available at your local pet store, and the care requirements for many of them will be similar. One of the main differences in keeping the different species of snakes is size. The attainable size of an adult snake should be the primary consideration in choosing a new pet. There are several smaller snake species that are readily available and make great choices for beginners.

Monty Krizan of
Monty's Traveling Reptile Show

All snakes are predators. This means every pet snake will require some type of animal as food. Most snakes commonly kept as pets will eat whole mice or rats. If you or someone in your household is uncomfortable with feeding snakes live or frozen/thawed food items weekly, then a snake is not the best choice for you. Keeping snakes successfully will depend on setting up the appropriate habitat and maintaining proper temperatures. The lifespan of snakes vary with species, however many snakes can live 5 to 10 years. Ball pythons can live 15 years or more if cared for properly. This means purchasing a snake can be a long-term commitment.

Snake Diversity

Snakes play a very important role in nature and are found on every continent except Antarctica. These unique animals range in size from the miniscule 5 inch Worm Snake from Northern Africa, to the longest snake on record: a 33 foot Reticulated Python from Indonesia. Snakes live in a variety of different habitats including: tropical rainforests, temperate forests, open plains and savannahs, scrublands, deserts, high in the mountains, deep underground and even in the oceans! Snakes live a secretive life and will avoid danger at all costs. All snakes are predators and eat a wide variety of prey. Many snakes feed on rodents, others specialize on lizards, frogs, eggs, birds, fish, large mammals, and some even specialize on other snakes. Of the many beautiful snakes in the world, a select few make great pets for the beginning snake keeper.

Excellent Choices for Beginners:

- Corn Snake   • Rosy Boa   • Garter Snake   • Milk Snake
- Ball Python   • Sand Boa   • Kingsnake

Excellent Choices for Intermediate Keepers:

These snakes have care requirements that make them more challenging, and are not recommended as beginner snakes.

- Red-tailed Boa Constrictor   • Rainbow Boa
- Green Tree Python   • Western Hognose Snake

Species that are difficult to maintain and are only recommended for the most advanced keepers:

- Blood Python
- Burmese Python
- Reticulated Python

Species Profiles

Snakes Suited for Beginners:

Corn Snakes/Rat Snakes

Common Name: Corn Snake or Red Rat Snake
Scientific Name: *Elaphe guttata*
Distribution: Eastern to Central U.S.
Size: 3'- 6'
Life Span: 10-15+ yrs.
Keeper Level: Beginner

Quick Tips: Corn Snakes are beautiful snakes with a gentle disposition. Over the years, captive breeding of this species has created an amazing variety of color morphs that are now available to beginning hobbyists. Corn Snakes are a type of Rat Snake. Rat Snakes have similar care requirements; however they will generally grow larger than Corn Snakes. There are several stories about how they were given the name "Corn" Snake; some say the checkered belly pattern looks like Indian corn, some say they were the 'Good' snakes to have in your corn field, and others say they were commonly found by farmers in barns where corn was being stored. They enjoy the shelter that barns create, and the mice and rats that are attracted to the corn.

Kingsnakes & Milk Snakes

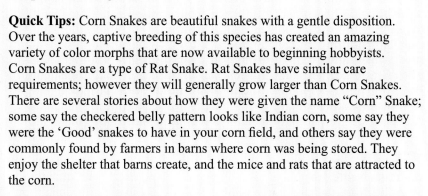

Common Name: Common Kingsnake, Common Milk Snake
Scientific Name: *Lampropeltis getula, Lampropeltis triangulum*
Distribution: Found throughout the eastern & southern U.S., west into California.
Size: 2.5'-5'+
Life Span: 5-12+ yrs.
Keeper Level: Beginner

Quick Tips: Kingsnakes and Milk Snakes are closely related and are among the most beautiful snakes in the world. These snakes have been popular pets in the reptile hobby since the beginning. There are many different types of

Milk and Kingsnakes found in North America, and care requirements are very similar for most of them. They are considered "Kings" because they regularly eat other species of snakes in the wild, including Rattlesnakes! Do not house multiple Kingsnakes or Milk Snakes together because they may eat each other. Kingsnakes eat a variety of prey in the wild including frogs, lizards, rodents, and snakes. It is recommended to offer your Kingsnake appropriately sized mice as a staple diet (see feeding section, pg. 13).

Ball Python

Common Name: Ball or Royal Python
Scientific Name: *Python regius*
Distribution: Western African countries
of Ghana, Togo, and Benin
Size: 3-5.5 ft.+
Life Span: 10-16+ yrs.
Keeper Level: Beginner

Quick Tips: Ball Pythons are an excellent beginner snake and one of the most popular pet snakes due to their docile nature. Captive bred Ball Pythons are becoming more readily available in the hobby, and the many color morphs being created have added to the growing popularity of this small python species. Ball Pythons were given the name "Ball" because when threatened, they will curl into a ball and hide their head in their coils. Ball pythons specialize on rodents in nature, making rats and mice a good food choice throughout their lives. Females will grow larger than males in this species, so if space is limited, we recommend purchasing a male.

Rosy Boa

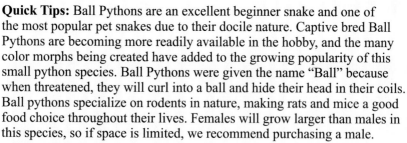

Common Name: Rosy Boa
Scientific Name: *Charina trivirgata*
Distribution: Southwest U.S., Baja &
Northern Mexico
Size: 2-3+ ft.
Life Span: 6-10+ yrs.
Keeper Level: Beginner

Quick Tips: Rosy Boas are among the best pet snakes to start with. This interesting snake is relatively easy to maintain and is very docile. Rosy Boas are among the smallest members of the Boa family (Boidae). These great snakes are available in a variety of colors and morphs. Rosy Boas come from dry habitats and will do best in a dry environment. These snakes will require pinkies or small mice as food throughout life. Feed Rosy Boas outside their cage to discourage aggressive feeding behaviors. Please do not collect Rosy Boas from the wild. There are many breeders working with this species, making it easy to find captive bred animals.

Garter Snakes

Common Name: Common Garter Snakes
Scientific Name: *Thamnophis sp.*
Distribution: Found throughout the U.S.
Size: 2'-4.5'
Life Span: 3-6+ yrs.
Keeper Level: Beginner

Quick Tips: There are many beautiful species of Garter Snakes that can be kept as pets. We recommend purchasing captive bred animals. Research your local wildlife laws because some Garter Snakes are protected. Garter Snakes are small snakes that eat small prey. This can be a challenge for beginning hobbyist because sometimes small food items can be difficult to find at a pet store. What Garter Snakes eat depends on the species and size, but most will accept feeder fish (some will even eat canned tuna!), pieces of fish fillet, chopped worms, frogs, toads and mice or pinkies. Some Garter Snakes may be difficult to feed, so we recommend offering a variety of food items to your snake. Make sure the snake of your choice is feeding on a readily accessible food before making a purchase. Garter Snakes can 'musk' people as a defense when being handled. The 'musk' is foul smelling but harmless. **We do not recommend the purchase of any "Asian" species of Garter Snakes as these can be "Rear Fanged" (venomous).**

Snakes Suited for Intermediate Keepers:

Red-Tailed Boa

Common Name: Red-Tailed Boa
Scientific Name: *Boa constrictor*
Distribution: Central and South America
Size: 3-10+ ft.
Life Span: 15-25 years
Keeper Level: Intermediate

Quick Tips: The Red-Tailed Boa is among the most common and well known species of snakes kept as pets. The common name Red-Tailed boa refers to one of many types of boas found throughout Central and South America. These snakes can grow to a large but manageable size and are recommended only for keepers with experience and who are willing to provide adequate space for adults. The friendly demeanor and attractive coloration have made the Red-Tailed boa one of the most sought after snakes in the hobby. These tropical snakes are commonly bred in captivity and we recommend purchasing captive bred animals only. Please remember to never release your pets into nature.

Rainbow Boa

Common Name: Rainbow Boa
Scientific Name: *Epicrates cenchria*
Distribution: Throughout tropical South America
Size: 4-6 ft.
Life Span: 15-25 years
Keeper Level: Intermediate to Advanced

Quick Tips: Rainbow Boas are considered one of the world's most beautiful snakes. These boas live mostly a terrestrial life, but will venture into trees in search of food. Rainbow Boas inhabit tropical rainforests and will need high levels of humidity (70%+). We recommend mixing Forest Floor™ and Eco Earth® together to create the ultimate moisture holding substrate for these forest boas. Maintaining humidity will be very important to keep these beautiful snakes healthy. Rainbow Boas are best left to keepers with experience because they can be aggressive, and their need for tropical conditions make them a bit more challenging than other species.

Green Tree Python

Common Name: Green Tree Python
Scientific Name: *Morelia viridis*
Distribution: Indonesia and surrounding Islands & Northern Australia
Size: 3-6+ ft.
Life Span: 10-15 yrs.
Keeper Level: Intermediate to Advanced

Quick Tips: Green Tree Pythons are recommended for intermediate to advanced keepers. These snakes are arboreal (live in trees) and will benefit from vertically oriented cages with plenty of sturdy climbing branches. This snake has a fragile skeleton, and is not recommended for frequent handling. Many experts that work with this species try not to handle hatchlings or juveniles at all. A removable perch will allow you to remove your snake without handling it. In the wild, Green Tree Pythons will eat a variety of prey including birds. We recommend offering your Green Tree Python appropriately sized mice.

*Note: *Juveniles are yellow and turn green as they get older.*

Blood, Burmese, Reticulated Pythons

Some species of snakes grow exceptionally large, and will quickly outgrow even the largest enclosures. The larger species of pythons and boas are only recommended for the most advanced keepers. Snakes such as the Burmese Python, Reticulated Python, African Rock Python and Anaconda are very attractive as hatchlings, however they will quickly grow into massive snakes requiring very large food items. The size of these snakes makes them very difficult to house properly and they have the potential to inflict serious injuries on keepers. These are best left to the most experienced herpetoculturists. We do not recommend the following species:

Anaconda

Burmese Python

Two Reticulated Pythons over 22 ft.
Courtesy of Monty Krizan

Selecting a Snake

The first goal in choosing a snake is deciding what species is most appropriate for you. Once you have researched the species you are interested in, choosing a healthy snake is easy. Below are some tips for selecting a healthy snake.

We recommend purchasing captive bred snakes whenever possible. Captive bred animals tend to have fewer parasites and eating problems, are less stressed in a captive environment, and are usually more docile. There are many breeders throughout the country that produce high-quality animals that make a great choice for beginning snake keepers. Any quality pet store will offer captive bred animals to their customers. Always ask information about where the snake came from and what it has been eating.

Look for Snakes:	Avoid Snakes:
Active and Alert	Unresponsive or lethargic
Flick their tongue regularly	Open mouth, wheezing, runny or bubbly nose
Usually round in shape	V-Shaped bodies or indentations along the sides
Free of old shed skin around the eyes and vent	With old scars and scabs. Free of ticks and mites. Saggy skin, flaky scales, dirty vent area
Has eaten in the past 2 weeks (ask the seller for details on feeding history)	Has not eaten for the seller in 3+ weeks
Captive Bred	Wild Caught

The Terrarium

A young Gopher snake in a dry desert terrarium.

Snake terrariums can range from a very simple glass tank set-up to an elaborate custom display cage. Whichever type of terrarium you choose for your snake, the key elements will remain the same; snakes need access to heat, shelter, water and food. The habitat you create will depend on which species you keep, but in general snakes will fall into one of two categories: Tropical or Desert habitat types. The difference in these tank set-ups will be the amount of humidity required (high humidity in tropical habitats, low humidity in desert habitats). The ecology, or lifestyle of the snake will determine the style of terrarium to be offered. Most snakes outlined in this book live a terrestrial life. Terrestrial species spend most of their time on the ground and in shallow burrows or rock crevices (i.e. Kingsnakes, Milk Snakes, Rosy Boas, Ball Pythons, Garter Snakes, Sand Boas). These terrestrial species will need a horizontally oriented cage, similar to that of a standard glass terrarium. Other snakes live in trees and are considered arboreal (i.e. Green Tree Pythons, Green Snakes). Arboreal snakes will need a vertically oriented terrarium with plenty of sturdy branches for climbing. Regardless of what type of snake you keep, all snake cages need to be escape-proof, preferably with a locking door. Snakes have the ability to re-arrange their enclosure, so make sure all cage furniture is secure so it can not fall and injure your snake.

Terrarium Size

Hatchling and Juveniles (up to 20") of most beginner species outlined above can be maintained in a 10 or 20 gallon terrarium. Bigger is not always better when it comes to housing young snakes. Small enclosures with plenty of hiding areas create the perfect habitat for baby snakes. Always provide a thick (2"+) layer of substrate for burrowing under. Young snakes can become stressed if kept in too large or open of a cage.

Snakes are escape artists, and any terrarium housing snakes needs to close securely, and preferably have a lock.

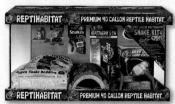

Zoo Med's Naturalistic® Terrarium comes in four sizes, and is appropriate for many hatchling and juvenile snakes, as well as adults of some small species (i.e. Sand Boas, Rosy Boas, Garter Snakes).

Zoo Med's ReptiHabitat Snake Kit comes with the essentials you will need to set up a new snake terrarium (20 and 40 gal).

NT-TL
Naturalistic®
Terrarium Repti Lock

Snake Terrarium Checklist

Below is a list of elements that make up a typical snake habitat.

Basic Elements of a Snake Habitat

- Terrarium
- Substrate
- Water Dish
- Under Tank Heater
- Shelter or Hide
- Thermometers
- Supplemental Heat (Heat Lamps)

Temperature

One of the most important aspects of successfully keeping snakes is providing heat for thermoregulation. Thermoregulation is a term used to describe how snakes maintain their body temperature. Reptiles are ectothermic, more commonly known as 'cold-blooded,' meaning their body temperature is dependent on the temperature of the environment around them. Different species of snakes will require different basking and ambient temperatures, so make sure you research the specific needs of your snake. Most snakes will need a basking area with temperatures between 82-95°F. Snakes will use behaviors such as seeking a warm basking site under the sun, or finding sun baked rocks to raise their body temperature. Other behaviors like retreating underground or seeking shelter are used to cool down. Snakes maintain their body temperature by regulating these behaviors between hot and cold environments. In herpetoculture, we achieve this by creating a 'thermal gradient'. Establishing a thermal gradient within your enclosure is essential for all reptiles. Although the term thermal gradient sounds complicated, it is actually quite simple to achieve. A gradient can be accomplished by providing heat on one side of the terrarium, and offering a cool shelter on the other. The difference in temperatures from one side of the enclosure to the other will create the perfect thermal gradient. Providing a warm and a cool place within the terrarium will allow your snake to thermoregulate. If your snake spends most of its time in the warm area, it could mean your terrarium temperatures are too low, conversely; if your snake spends most of its time in the cool area, it could mean your terrarium is too warm. Always use a quality thermometer to monitor your temperatures.

The photo to the right shows the basic idea of a thermal gradient. By offering a warm basking area on the left and a cool area on the right, a gradient is established.

Types of Heating Elements

Of the many different types of heating devices available, the most important for snakes will be an Under Tank Heater such as Zoo Med's ReptiTherm® UTH Heater. The ReptiTherm® provides what we call 'belly heat'. Belly heat is heat from the bottom of the cage that the snake can lay on. Belly heat is very important for maintaining body temperature and for digestion. The ReptiTherm® UTH is designed to be used with substrate to distribute heat evenly.

Other types of heat commonly offered to snakes are from overhead heat sources such as a heat lamp. The Repti Basking Spot™ Lamp or Daylight Blue™ Bulb can be used for daytime heat, and the Infrared Nocturnal Heat Lamp or Nightlight Red™ Bulb can be used for nighttime heat. Zoo Med offers an entire line of both day and night heat lamps, some that will create a basking spot by projecting light downward (Repti Basking Spot™ Lamp/ Infrared Nocturnal Lamp), and other types that are great for supplemental heat to maintain ambient temperatures (Daylight Blue™/ Nightlight Red™).

Other types of heating elements commonly used for snakes include Ceramic Heat Emitters, Repti Heat Cable™, and Heat Rocks. Ceramic Heat emitters are a great way to provide heat, but care must be taken that snakes do not have direct access to the emitter. We always recommend using the Ceramic Heat Emitter with a Wire Cage Clamp Lamp. Zoo Med's ReptiCare® Rock Heaters are a great way to offer supplemental belly heat to your snake. However, these heating devices should never be the sole source of heat available to your snake. Zoo Med's ReptiCare® Heat Rocks are specially designed to distribute heat evenly throughout the rock, thus avoiding potential burns from a 'hot-spot'.

It is very important to monitor temperatures at both ends of your cage using a quality Zoo Med Thermometer. **Know your terrarium temperatures, don't guess!**

Regulating Heat and Monitoring Temperature

Many of Zoo Med's heating elements can be regulated with a ReptiTemp™ Rheostat or ReptiTemp™ Digital Thermostat. Always use a quality thermometer to monitor temperatures such as Zoo Med's Digital Thermometer or Analog Thermometer. There are three important temperatures to monitor in your terrarium: the Basking Spot (Hot Spot), Ambient (overall air temperature or room temp.), and the cool spot. We recommend having a thermometer at least in the hot an areas of your terrarium.

Lighting

Due to the fact that snakes eat whole food items such as rodents, it is believed that snakes receive the needed nutrients and calcium from their diet. It has been

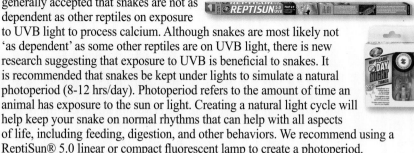

generally accepted that snakes are not as dependent as other reptiles on exposure to UVB light to process calcium. Although snakes are most likely not 'as dependent' as some other reptiles are on UVB light, there is new research suggesting that exposure to UVB is beneficial to snakes. It is recommended that snakes be kept under lights to simulate a natural photoperiod (8-12 hrs/day). Photoperiod refers to the amount of time an animal has exposure to the sun or light. Creating a natural light cycle will help keep your snake on normal rhythms that can help with all aspects of life, including feeding, digestion, and other behaviors. We recommend using a ReptiSun® 5.0 linear or compact fluorescent lamp to create a photoperiod.

Substrate

Substrate is a term used to describe the type of 'bedding' used on the cage floor. There are many types of bedding that are suitable for snakes. Choosing the right bedding for your snake will depend on the species and where it lives. The different types of bedding available will all have different water-holding properties. Some snakes live in wet rainforests and others live in the desert. These different environments need to be re-created for your snake. The most preferred type of bedding for snakes in general is Zoo Med's Aspen Snake Bedding. This finely milled Aspen is very clean and allows smaller snakes to create burrows. Aspen Snake Bedding is very easy to 'spot clean' and has natural odor absorbing properties. For snakes that live in moist environments, Zoo Med's Forest Floor™ Cypress bedding is a great choice (i.e. Rainbow Boa). Cypress bedding will hold moisture and help maintain humidity within the terrarium. It is important to remember that although a snake may live in an arid environment such as a desert, they spend much of their time in rock crevices or deep underground where temperatures tend to be cooler with higher humidity. Some desert species, such as the Kenyan Sand Boa will prefer sand substrates such as ReptiSand® or ReptiFresh®. Zoo Med's Excavator® Clay Substrate can be used to create underground burrows and dens that your desert species will love! In the wild, most snakes do not dig their own burrow, instead they choose to use burrows made by rodents and other animals.

Mix Zoo Med's Eco Earth® and Forest Floor™ Bedding to create the ultimate tropical snake bedding. This mix will hold moisture and help maintain humidity in tropical terrariums.*

Cedar & Redwood

CAUTION: Some types of wood can be toxic to snakes and should never be used in a snake enclosure. Woods to stay away from are redwood, eucalyptus and cedar. Any wood that has a strong fragrance most likely contains resins or saps that may be toxic to snakes and other reptiles. *

Shelter

It is essential to provide a shelter for your snake to retreat and seek cover. Snakes make use of underground retreats for shelter from the elements and from predators. Your snake should be able to completely fit inside its shelter. Snakes are secretive animals and will choose to avoid danger at all costs. Providing a shelter will help reduce stress and make your snake feel secure in its home. A ReptiShelter™ is a great way to provide cover, and can be filled with New Zealand Sphagnum Moss to create a humidity chamber. A 'humidity chamber' is a shelter that holds moistened moss and is offered to create a humid environment that will help your snake as it sheds its skin. Other shelters can be used such as a Habba Hut™, Cork Rounds or Mopani Wood. Anything that a snake can retreat to and feel safe is an adequate shelter. We recommend having a shelter on both the warm and cool sides of your terrarium to allow your snake to regulate its body temperature in security. Shelters also offer a rough surface that your snake will use to help shed its skin. Shelters and other cage décor such as Natural Bush Plants will help break sightlines. A sight line describes the ability of an animal to see through its enclosure. By breaking this sight line with cage décor, you will create more security for your pet.

Food

Snakes eat a variety of different animals in nature, and do so in one-amazingly large mouthful! Snakes have the ability to disarticulate (dislocate) their jaw bones, allowing them to swallow prey up to 5 times larger than their head! All snakes eat single, whole meals without the need or ability to chew. Watching a snake capture and eat its prey is one of the most amazing feats in nature that you can experience right in your home! What a snake eats in nature will depend on the species, the age, and the time of year. For the snake species described in this book, we recommend offering rodents, such as mice or rats. These types of 'feeders' are easy to find at your local pet store and have all the ingredients of a well-rounded snake diet.

In nature, snakes need to take advantage of food when it is available and they will sometimes go very long periods of time without food. Snakes usually will eat one meal that can last them a week or longer. This means most pet snakes will only need to be offered food once a week.

Rodents can be offered alive or dead. Many stores offer frozen rodents that make feeding your snake easy. Any frozen food item needs to be completely thawed before offering to your snake. When thawing out vertebrate prey (i.e. frozen mice), it is best to slowly thaw the item over 24 hours in a refrigerator; the item may be brought to room temperature after thawing completely if desired. This method greatly reduces the possibility of bacterial contamination. Live food gives your snake the opportunity to hunt and exercise, however never leave your snake alone with a live rodent. Rodents can attack, and even kill a snake if the snake is not interested in eating at the time.

Snakes can become aggressive towards the keeper if they are fed inside the enclosure. Because of this, we recommend removing your snake from its enclosure for all feedings. Place your snake in a plastic container, box, or paper bag containing the food item. After your snake has finished its meal, gently place the snake back into its enclosure. Take care while handling your snake because it will have a full belly. It is not recommended to handle any snake for a few days after eating.

Size of food/Diagram

We recommend feeding your snake a food item that is no wider than the width of its head.

Measure by widest part of food item.

Feeding Problems

One of the most challenging aspects of keeping snakes is dealing with feeding problems. It is natural for some snakes to 'go off' food periodically throughout the year, and this may be the simple reason your snake is not eating. Most often when snakes stop feeding, it is due to cool temperatures or stress. The first thing to do when your snake refuses to eat is to check your temperatures. The warm side of the cage and the basking spot must be maintained at a minimum of 82°F degrees. Snakes without access to a warm area in the cage will not accept food because the temperatures are not adequate for digestion. Without heat, snakes will slowly develop respiratory infections or become susceptible to other ailments or diseases.

Tips for Problem Feeders: Place the food item in a paper bag with the snake (preferably frozen/thawed). Sometimes snakes can be stressed from activity around the cage. By placing the food item in a paper bag you can reduce stress by eliminating sight lines.

• Try offering food late at night.

• Try offering food during storms. Snakes can sense the change in pressure of the atmosphere and this can entice them to feed.

Water

Providing fresh, clean water daily is essential for caring for your snake. Snakes, like most reptiles, need constant access to clean fresh water. Tap water throughout the country may be contaminated with chlorine,

chloramines, heavy metals and other toxins. We recommend treating all tap water with ReptiSafe® Water Conditioner. ReptiSafe® removes these contaminants from tap water while adding beneficial electrolytes.

Make sure your water bowl is not placed over an Under Tank Heater, or directly under a heat lamp. In general, we recommend keeping water bowls on the cool end of the cage. For most snake species, the water bowl should be large enough that the snake can fit its entire body in to soak. Remember that your water bowl will be a source of humidity in your terrarium, meaning some desert species will do best with a smaller water bowl that they may not fit into (i.e. Rosy and Sand Boas), thus keeping relative humidity low. Relative humidity should be monitored with Zoo Med's Hygrometer. For tropical species that require high humidity, such as the Brazilian Rainbow Boa, and Green Tree Python, the ReptiFogger™ or ReptiRain® can be used to maintain high levels of humidity. The Environmental Control Center can be used with the ReptiFogger™ or the ReptiRain® to regulate and maintain a set humidity level.

Zoo Med's Corner Bowl is the preferred water bowl for most snake keepers. This bowl is made entirely of recycled plastic and snuggly fits into the corner of your terrarium. This corner design conserves space and is very difficult for your snake to tip over.

Handling

Handling snakes can be a fun way to interact with your pet. Snakes need to be handled with two hands. One hand is used to support the weight of the snake and should be positioned in the middle portion of the snake's body. The front hand can be used in a hand over hand motion that allows the handler to "be the branch". Your snake needs to feel secure, so support the weight of the snake's body at all times. Always watch your snake's behavior and be careful of sudden movements. Zoo Med's Snake Hook is a great tool used to handle small snakes of all kinds. It is recommended to keep your hands away from the head of the snake when possible. Always wash your hands after handling a pet rodent or small animal like a pet rat, hamster, rabbit, guinea pig etc., as your snake could interpret this scent as prey and bite you! The species outlined in this book are known as being very gentle snakes and most will not bite if unprovoked. If you do get bitten, try your hardest not to rip your hand away. Bites from these species are very mild, and should be cared for like a minor cut. Always wash your hands after handling your snake or cage furniture. We do not recommend wrapping your snake around your neck, or allowing your snake near your face. It is important to remember that not everyone likes snakes, and some people have a severe fear of snakes (Ophidiophobia). Please remember you have a responsibility as a snake owner to not make other people feel uncomfortable. We do not recommend walking with your snake in public places, because this can scare people and your snake.

Maintenance

Maintaining a snake cage is simple and can usually be accomplished in just a few minutes per week. Snakes will usually defecate (poop) less than most types of animals because they have a slow metabolism and eat less often. This makes 'spot-cleaning' a great method of maintaining the cleanliness of your terrarium. Spot Cleaning refers to a technique where the keeper removes solid waste and soiled bedding as it appears. Using the proper substrate will help absorb liquids and makes cleaning easier. Full substrate changes will be needed once every 3-4 weeks depending on the type and quantity of snakes being kept. Caging and cage furniture should be cleaned thoroughly with disinfectant such as Zoo Med's Wipe-Out 1™ Terrarium Cleaner.

Health

Of the common problems experienced by snake keepers, most are caused by inadequate temperatures and/or lack of sanitation. It is very important to establish a thermal gradient in your snake's cage (outlined on pg. 9). Providing your snake adequate temperatures will be the first step in keeping a healthy snake. It is very important to meet your local exotic animal veterinarian and develop a relationship with him or her. Veterinarians can be a great resource to learn about your snake and to offer support when there is a problem. Many of the health issues facing captive snakes are beyond the scope of this book, so we will explore only the most common ailments, and strongly recommend purchasing a good book on your species and seeking the advice of a veterinarian.

Shedding

As snakes grow, they will begin the process of shedding to remove old worn skin. You will notice your snake's eyes begin to turn a cloudy blue color several days before it sheds its skin. When you see the skin begin to turn blue, it is recommended you offer a humidity chamber (described on pg. 12). Zoo Med's Shedding Aid is a great treatment to help snakes shed properly. For some species, such as Ball pythons and Kingsnakes, we recommend misting the cage with water during this time. The increase in humidity will help your snake loosen its skin and prepare to shed. It is a good idea to offer a rock, or Mopani Wood to help your snake begin the shedding process. When it is time, your snake will rub against rough surfaces in the cage to begin the shed process. If your snake sheds in patches or retains skin over the head/eye region, it may be a sign your cage is too dry. If this happens, begin soaking your snake daily to help loosen and remove any unshed skin. Soaking snakes in tepid water for 30 minutes is a great way to help manage shedding problems.

Parasites

Sometimes snakes come into the pet trade with external parasites. Ticks and Mites are the most common parasites found on snakes. Ticks are easily removed manually with tweezers and a good soak. Soak your snake in tepid (warm) water for 30 minutes at a time, and repeat daily for a week. Most ticks will fall off your snake, and others will be easily removed.

Mites are more difficult to treat, and are considered one of the most challenging aspects in snake care. Mites are small black circular insects that look like poppy seeds. They are most common on wild caught snakes, and are usually found in the head region. Mites can often be found around the eyes and nostrils of the snake. Upon close inspection, small whitish mites (young mites) can be found running in and out from under the scales. Snake scales provide a perfect habitat for these parasites to be protected from the elements. Treating mites will take several weeks and can be very challenging. The first step is to remove your snake and soak it in tepid water. To do this, place your snake in a plastic container with a lid, filled with enough water to cover your snake completely, but make sure there is air available. Usually 2-3 inches of water is adequate. Soak your snake for up to 30 minutes while you are cleaning its enclosure. Remove all contents of the cage and thoroughly rinse and disinfect with Wipe-Out. While treating your cage, we recommend using paper towels or newspaper as a substrate because mites can lay their eggs in the substrate making it more difficult to manage. Repeat this procedure twice a week until you are sure that there are no longer mites on your snake.